Chakra Centers Creative Guide
Harness Your Chi Through Creativity

Written by Regina Marie Woodard
Illustrated by Legan Rooster

©2012, updated ©2021
Published by Bean Wing Books ©2024
ISBN 979-8-9921142-8-7

This book is dedicated to Sensei, Seekers, and Scholars who share their wisdom as teachers for the benefit of all.

THIS
BOOK
IS FOR

Immigrants, emigrants, and refugees of the self; all those who've traversed and travelled in search of home.

You are invited here to look within and find your way to the home that has always been inside of you and to immerse into the creative process as a form of centering, focusing, and allowing a deeper connection to consciousness.

CHI &
CREATIVE
FLOW

Allow yourself to express your creativity on these pages and connect to the subtle energy of your own body. Let these pages be the templates for the poetry within you to be painted, written, and expressed.

Many ideas for how to get creative with this book can be found on Instagram **@inthebright** and at **inthebright.com.** Love your whole self.

EVERYTHING IS ENERGY
& Energy is Everything

In many Eastern cultures the concept that everything is energy has been ingrained into the core beliefs and values for millennia. This Universal Energy is called Qi, Chi, Ki or Prana, depending upon the place of origin. In this book, I use the terms Qi and Chi (pronounced *chee*) interchangeably to denote this concept of Universal Lifeforce Energy. As humans have evolved by way of size and skin tone, culture and cuisine, language and religion, our perspectives and core beliefs have diverged as well. The idea of a Universal Qi Energy that makes up everything in physical universe and operates the cosmos is only recently becoming mainstream in the West as science and spirituality converge in the modern age. Physicists are confiming that all matter is energy, vibrating in open space, and into this space, a measurable magnetic field emits from the heart center; biologists are discovering more about epigenetics and the effect of emotions and memory on cells; quantum particles are being found to exist in two places at once. Science is catching up with what the ancients have taught, and with each discovery, we accept a little bit more and shift perspective. This notion that everything is energy vibrating is no longer theory, it's measurable and the modern perception of how the world works links back directly to the ancient wisdom of Qi.

THE CENTRAL ENERGY CHANNEL

The word "chakra" translates as wheel or disc from Sanskrit. Chakras are described as cyclones of energy that radiate out from a central energy channel in the core of the body. The spinal chakras begin at the coccyx, or tail bone, and run up the center of the body and out the top of the head. There are seven main physical chakras that run through the central channel of the body and correspond to nerve plexuses in the spine which control physical functions. These electro-magnetic energy centers are an extension of the nervous system, subtly managing the body's metabolism and regulating Qi. The chakras are not physical organs, but energetically connect the emotional and behavioral processing of the limbic system in the brain and endocrine system, which regulates gland secretion. At each chakra level, there are corresponding psychological functions, so that the chakras energetically metabolize our thoughts and emotions. Visually, the chakra system is represented by a full spectrum of visible light: a rainbow. Each chakra level represents an aspect of our own consciousness, so that the higher chakras fully open only when the affairs of the lower chakras are in order.

Anodea Judith, author of *Wheels of Life,* calls it, "a system for reclaiming our wholeness." By looking within, through the lenses of the chakras, individuals are able to function more fully in the world.

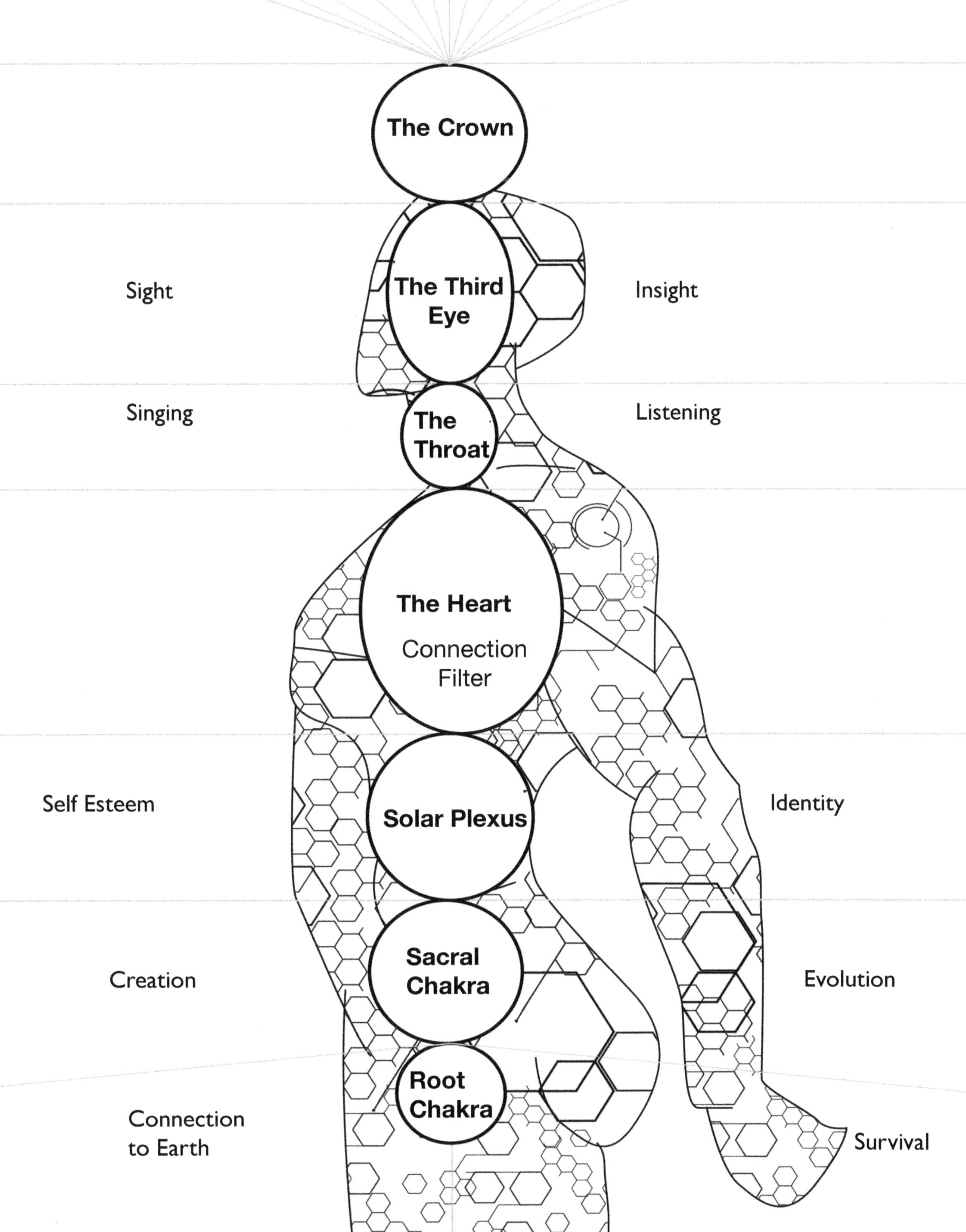

The Crown
The Third Eye
The Throat
The Heart
Connection Filter
Solar Plexus
Sacral Chakra
Root Chakra
Sight
Insight
Singing
Listening
Self Esteem
Identity
Creation
Evolution
Connection to Earth
Survival

GROUNDING EXERCISE
Tune in to the Root

Sit, stand or lay down so that you are comfortable.
Breathe. Feel yourself in your body and listen to your breath.

In your mind's eye visualize a column of sparkling light and iridescence shining down on you from the sky. This light comes down from above and in, through the top of your head, running through the core of your being. Imagine this light coming down through the spinal column and out of the last vertebra like a long tail. This energetic tail exiting out of your coccyx is your grounding cord. Visualize this cord as a root moving downward, towards the ground and into the cool nourishing earth below you. Let your grounding cord grow downward and fractal out like roots into the soil, down through the Earth's crust and mantle and to the center of the Earth. Any thoughts, emotions, or pain that is no longer serving you can be sent through the tail grounding cord to be composted by the Earth or burnt up in its molten center.

Breathe and visualize this column of energy coming from the sky through the top of your head and out your tailbone into the Earth. Connect to this cord of light and let it light you up from within. This sparkling column of light holds your essence.

Scan your body and shine your inner eye into the core of your body. Visualize the light coming from a prism, a beam of sunlight fractured into a perfect rainbow. Imagine the light is shining within and around you, as if you are the prism.

You can do this exercise anytime to center and connect to the creative flow of Qi.

MULADHARA
The Root Chakra

Survival and Connection to Earth

Color: Red
4 petal lotus

note: C
sound: Lam

Balance and Movement

Pleasure

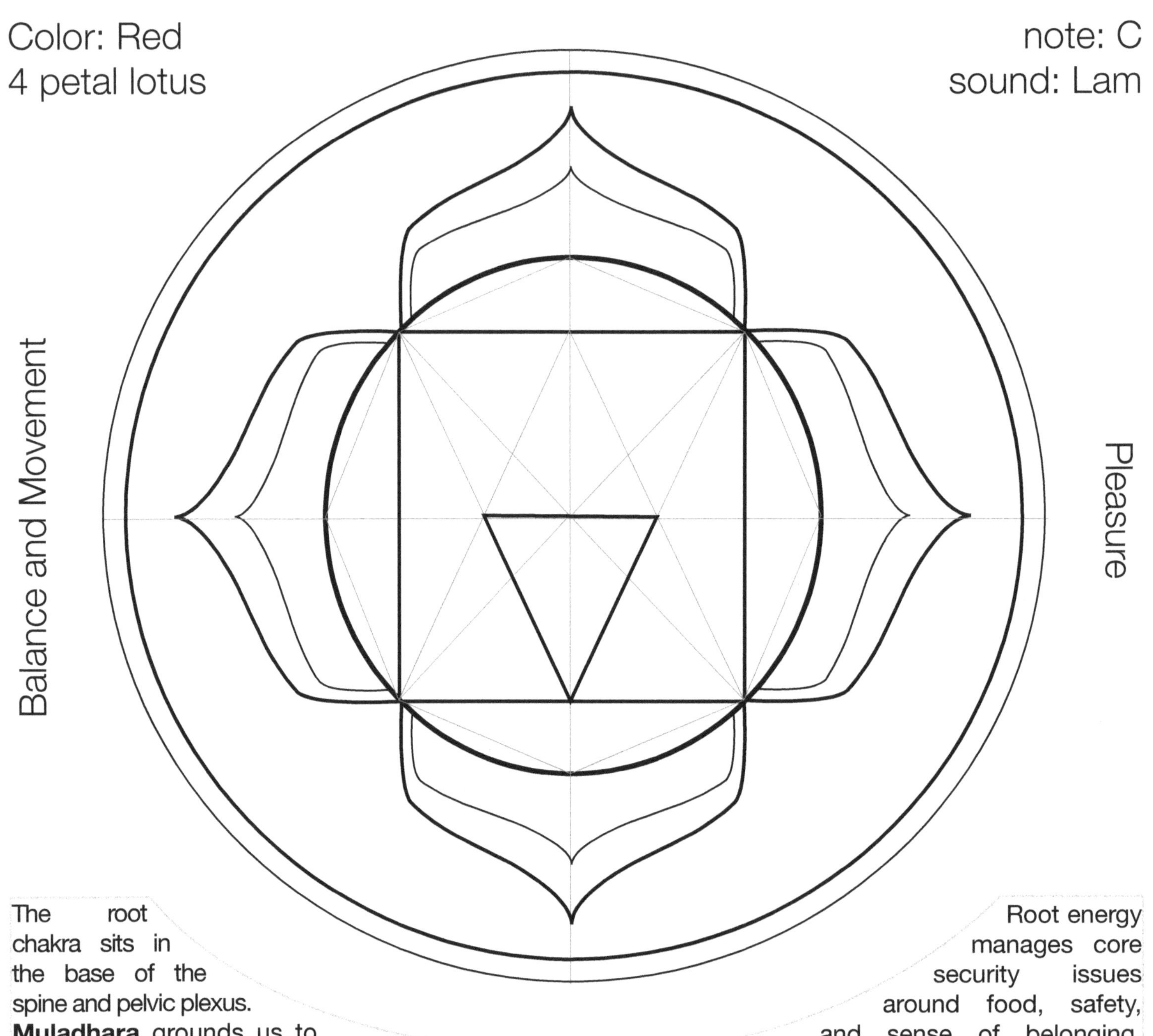

The root chakra sits in the base of the spine and pelvic plexus. **Muladhara** grounds us to Earth and links us to its magnetic field.
The root chakra is the link to physical life on Earth and relates to our basic needs and animal instincts. The first chakra oversees the bones and rectum and metabolizes the feelings of physical, emotional, and mental security.

Root energy manages core security issues around food, safety, and sense of belonging.

The core beliefs that develop based on the family, tribe, or culture that one is born into are held in the root chakra. The lowest chakra is the densest energetically and the closest to matter, linking physicality to the effects of atmosphere and gravity.

Security- Suguridad
Plenty -- Abundancia
Generosity -- Generosidad
Bumble bee sound. Abeja--BZZzzzzz

SVADHISTHANA
The Sacral Chakra

Creation and Evolution

Color: Orange
6 petal lotus

note: D
sound: Vam

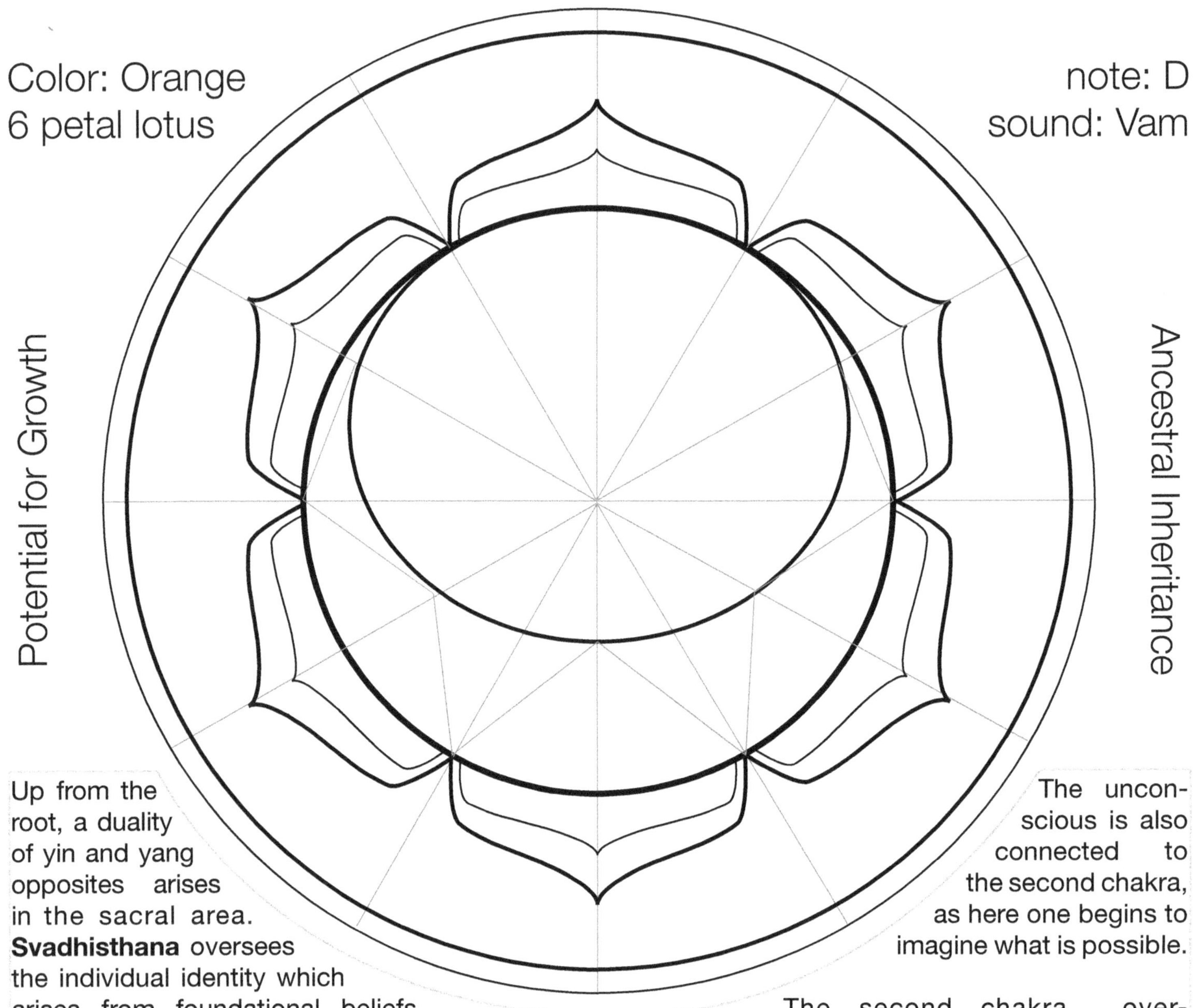

Up from the root, a duality of yin and yang opposites arises in the sacral area. **Svadhisthana** oversees the individual identity which arises from foundational beliefs held in the root chakra, opening the potential for movement and change.

The sacral chakra regulates the sex organs, reproduction, the pelvis, and prostate. Physically, it holds the gonads and gametes, the energy of pure creation. Symbolically, the lingam and yoni represent the polarity of opposites that come together to form new life: the force of divine duality to create.

The unconscious is also connected to the second chakra, as here one begins to imagine what is possible.

The second chakra oversees feelings about relationships, union with others and the creative forces of life.

Together the first and second chakras are also called the **secret chakras**. They fill the pelvic bowl and harness the individual to their center of gravity. These base chakras guide our most animal instincts and give birth to our highest aspirations.

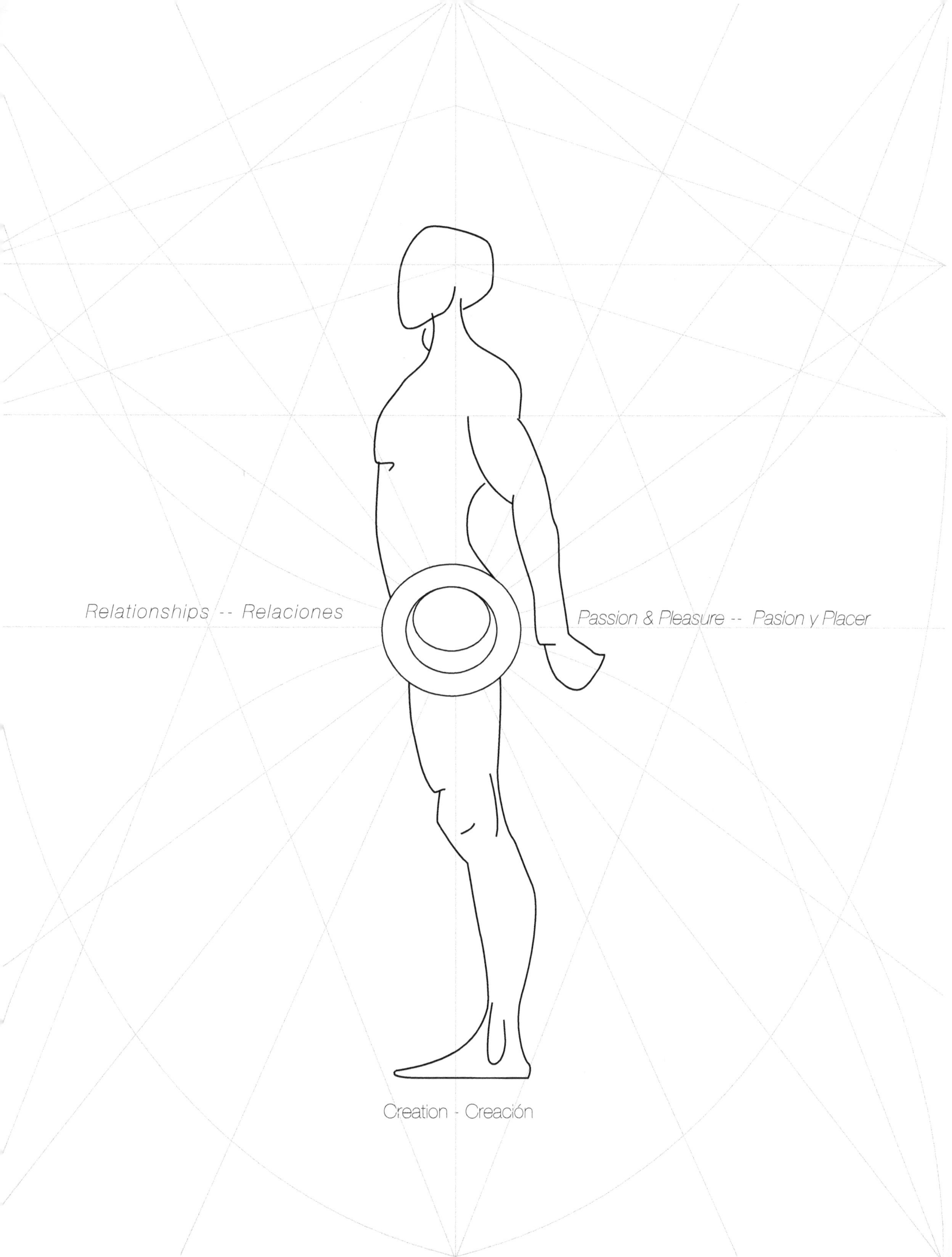

Relationships -- Relaciones
Passion & Pleasure -- Pasion y Placer
Creation - Creación

MANIPURA
The Solar Plexus

Self Identity and Esteem

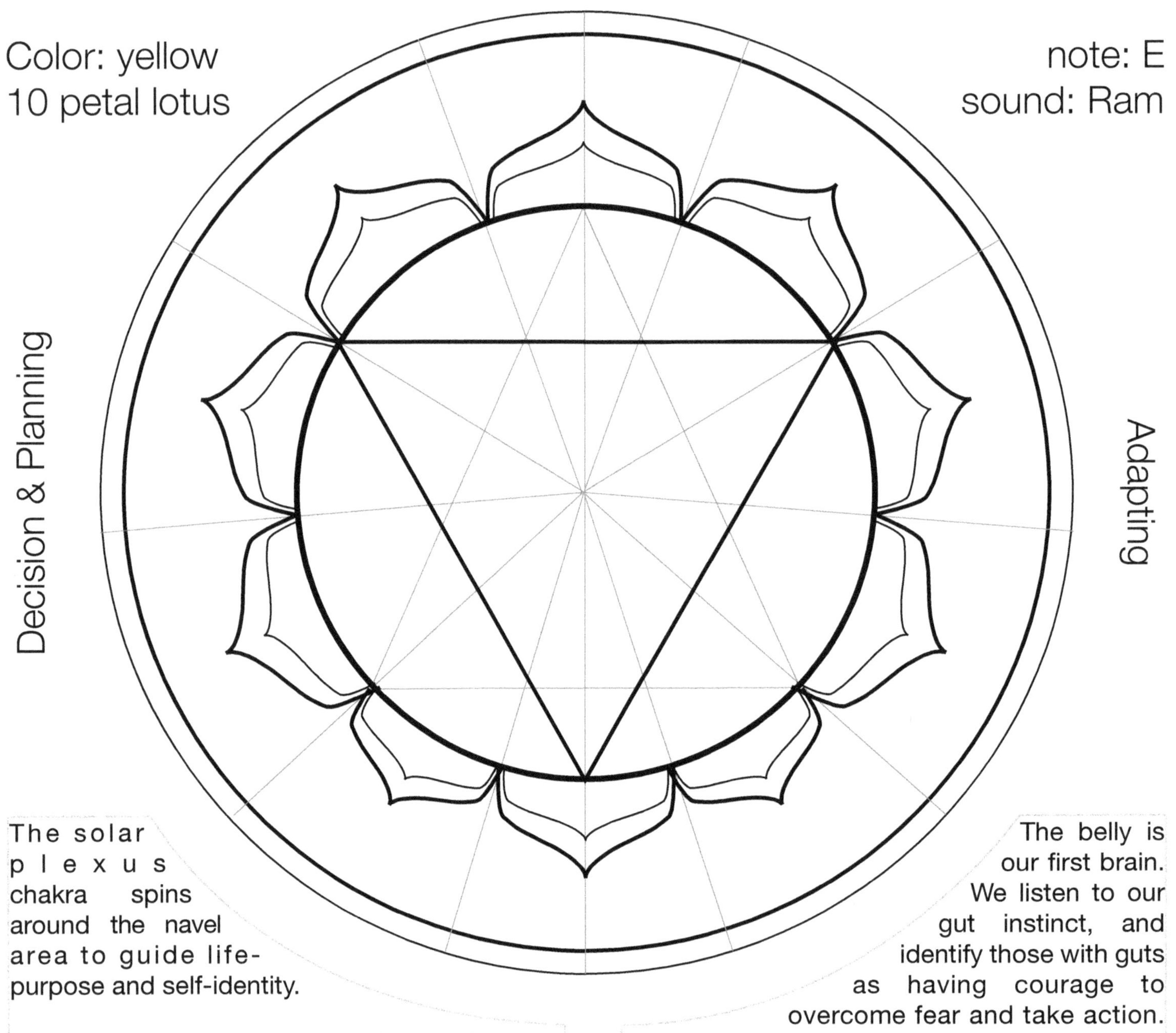

The solar plexus chakra spins around the navel area to guide life-purpose and self-identity.

Manipura rules over courage, fear and ego.

In the physical area of the solar plexus, food is digested and metabolized into electrical energy and matter. The products of digestion build the physical body with nutrients, and the electrical impulses of the heart move it into action, so it is here one exercises personal willpower.

The belly is our first brain. We listen to our gut instinct, and identify those with guts as having courage to overcome fear and take action.

In this way, the third chakra connects to self-esteem while self-control and integrity also develop in the area of the solar plexus.

The energy of birthright, ancestral connection and the digestion of personal destiny circulate around the area of the umbilicus.

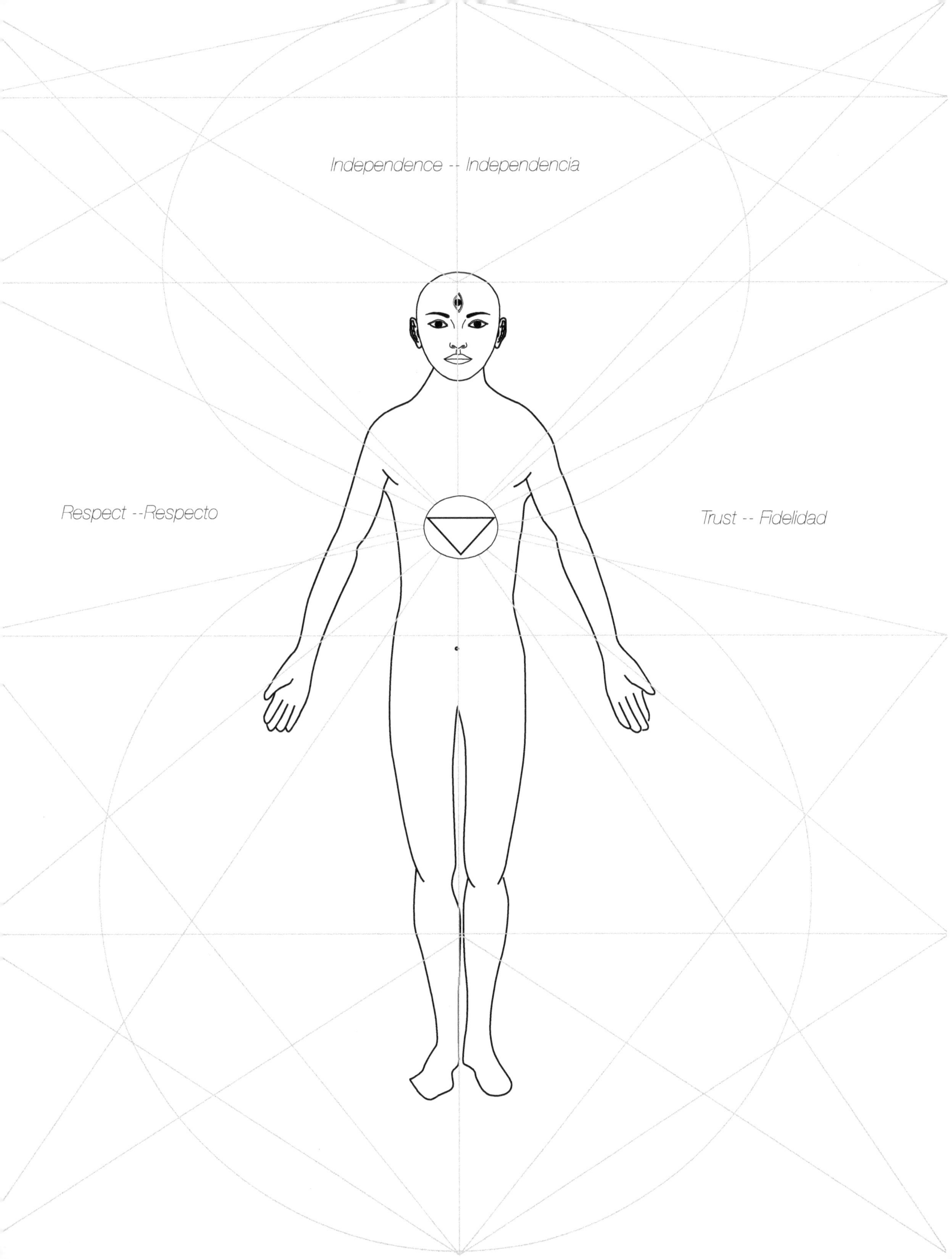

Independence -- Independencia
Respect --Respecto
Trust -- Fidelidad

ANAHATA
The Heart Chakra

Filter and Connection Between Heaven and Earth

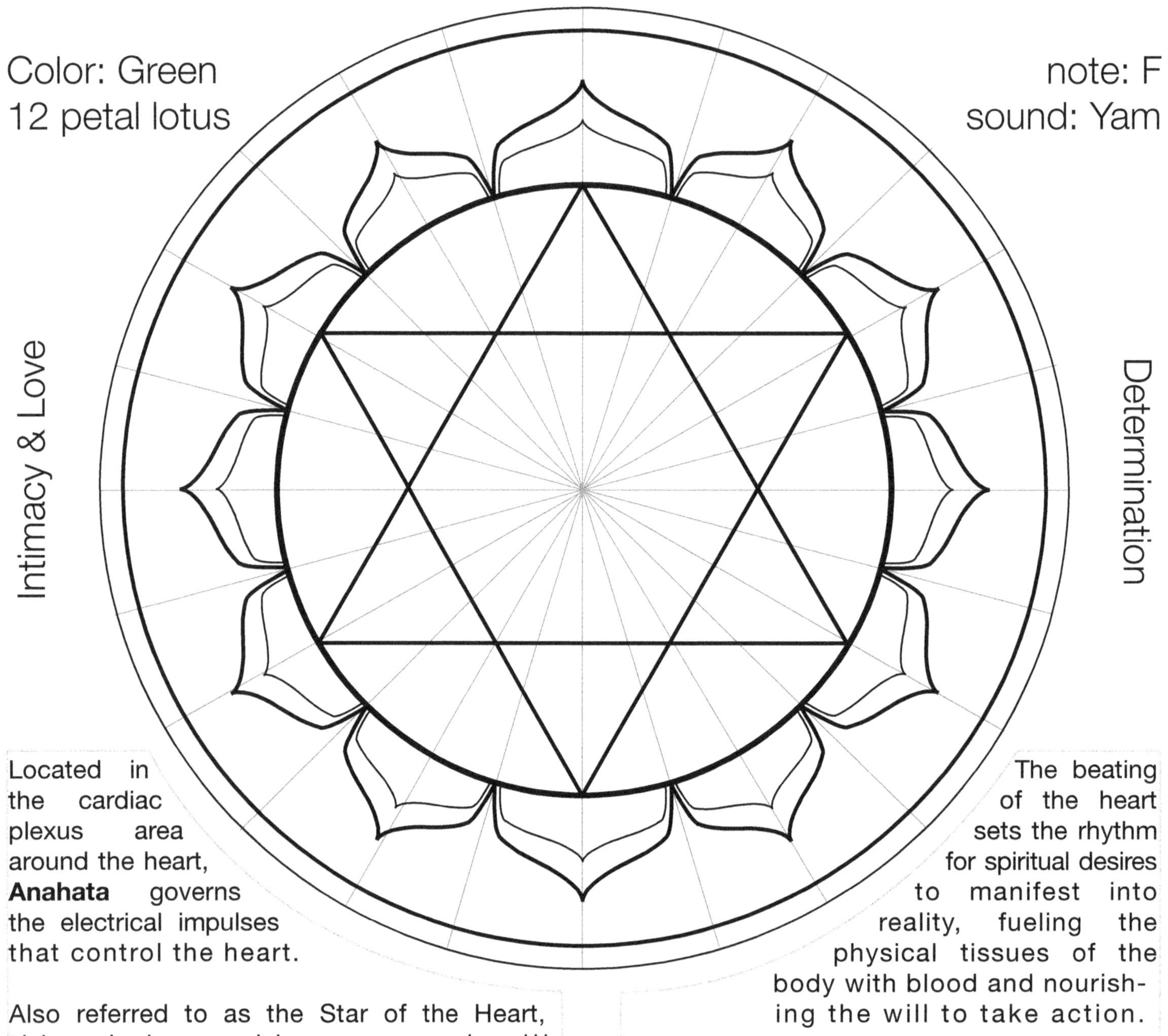

Located in the cardiac plexus area around the heart, **Anahata** governs the electrical impulses that control the heart.

Also referred to as the Star of the Heart, this chakra guides personal will.

The heart center is a meeting point between the material density of the lower three chakras and the lighter ethereal world of the upper three chakras. Physically this manifests as electrical impulses, causing the heart to beat, pumping blood throughout the physical body.

The beating of the heart sets the rhythm for spiritual desires to manifest into reality, fueling the physical tissues of the body with blood and nourishing the will to take action.

As the junction between the physical and etheric, the heart chakra serves as an inner temple where one contemplates personal desire by listening to the will of the heart. The heart center is the beginning of spiritual life, where the voice of higher consciousness can be heard by connecting to the heart center.

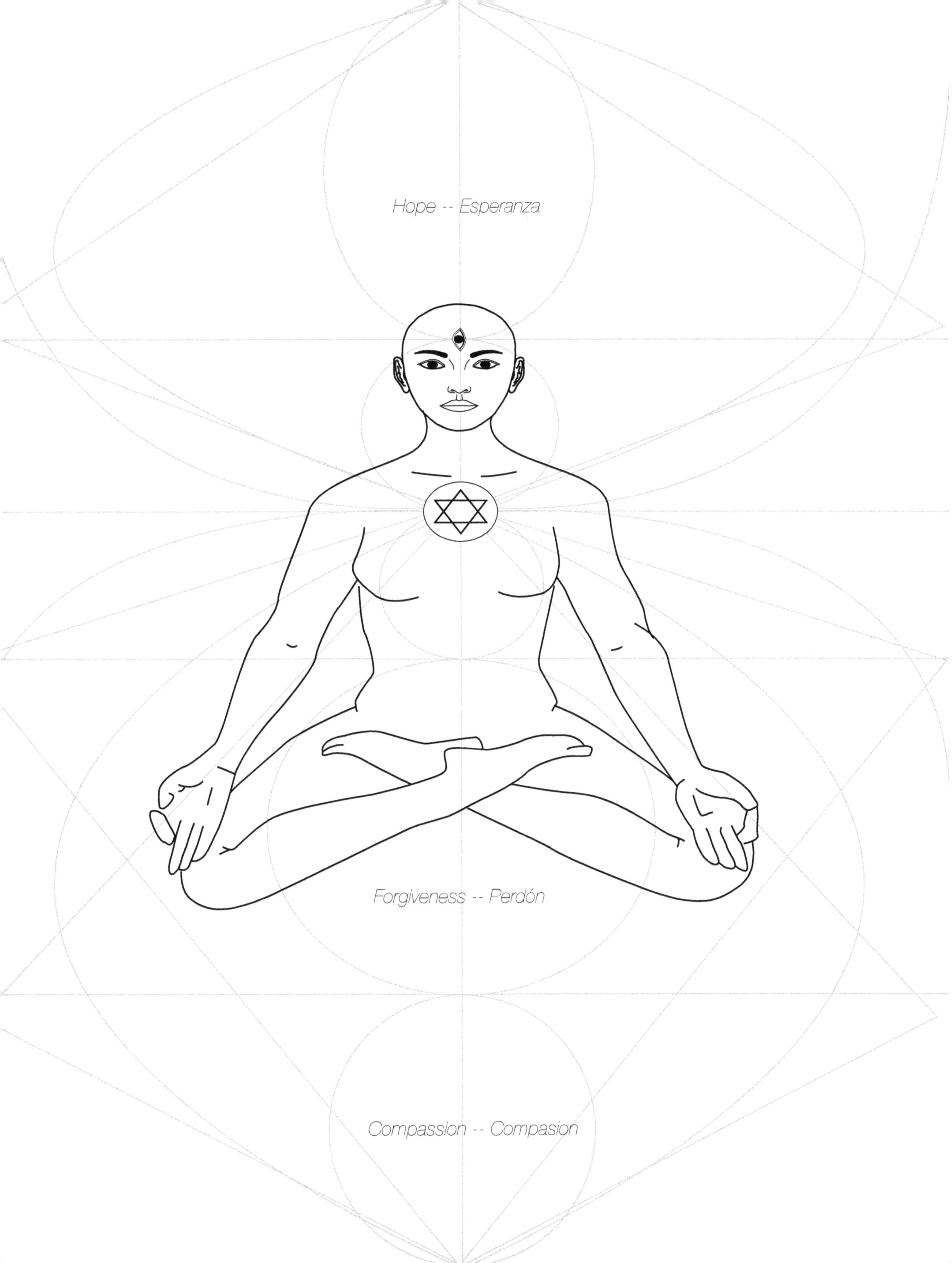

Hope -- Esperanza
Forgiveness -- Perdón
Compassion -- Compasion

VISHUDDHI
The Throat
Singing and Listening

Color: Blue
16 petal lotus

note: G
sound: Ham

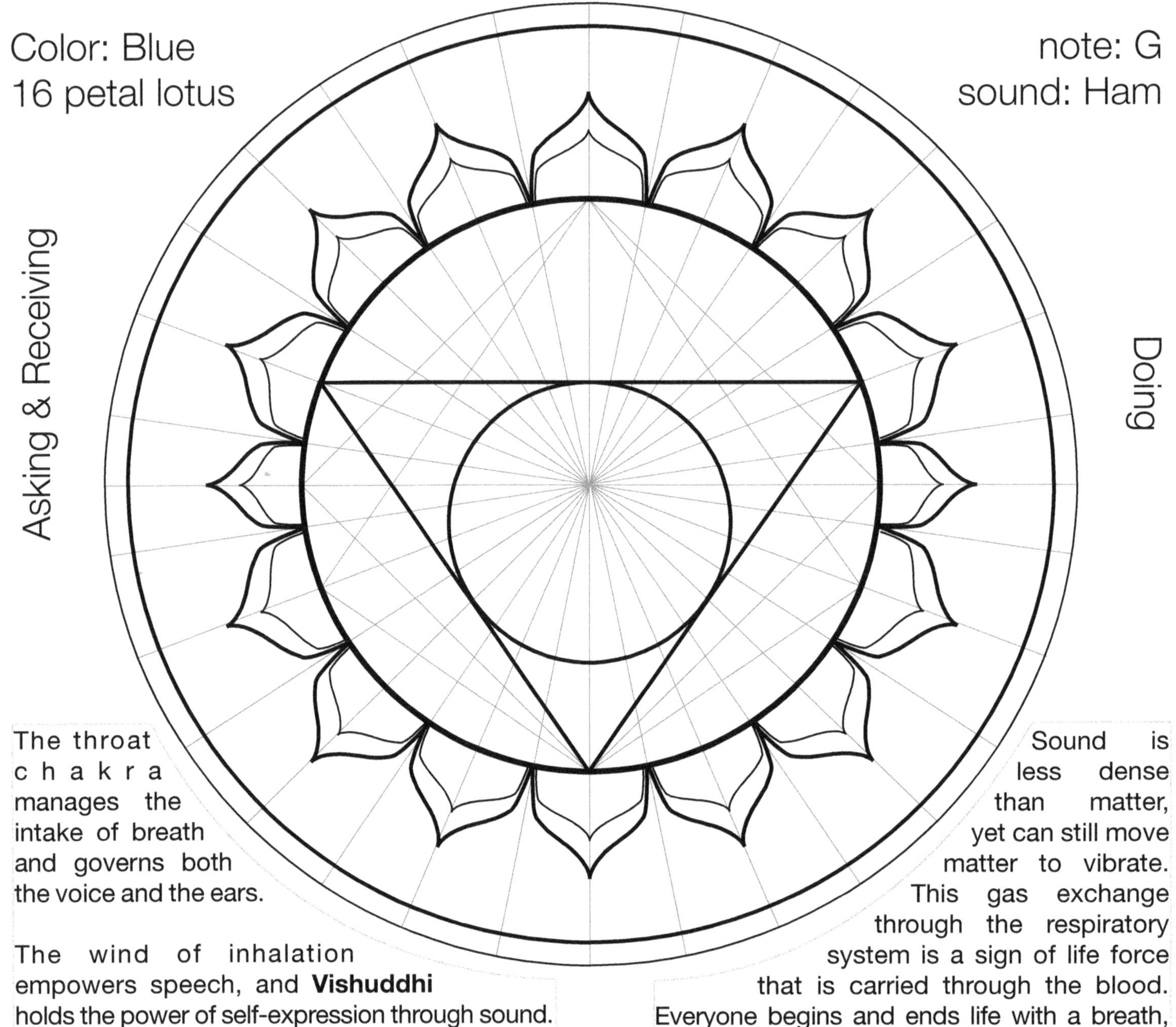

The throat chakra manages the intake of breath and governs both the voice and the ears.

The wind of inhalation empowers speech, and **Vishuddhi** holds the power of self-expression through sound.

Beliefs and intentions distilled in the lower chakras are expressed through speech at the throat area. Energetically, the throat chakra holds the key to manifestation, as the voice is the vehicle for expressing one's will, and the words one speaks create one's reality.

Sound is less dense than matter, yet can still move matter to vibrate. This gas exchange through the respiratory system is a sign of life force that is carried through the blood. Everyone begins and ends life with a breath, and the throat chakra invokes the life force of the invisible and expresses the will of the heart.

Both the power of mercy and judgment are seated in this chakra. Listening is the yin opposite of speaking and the two must be exercised equally to find understanding or truth.

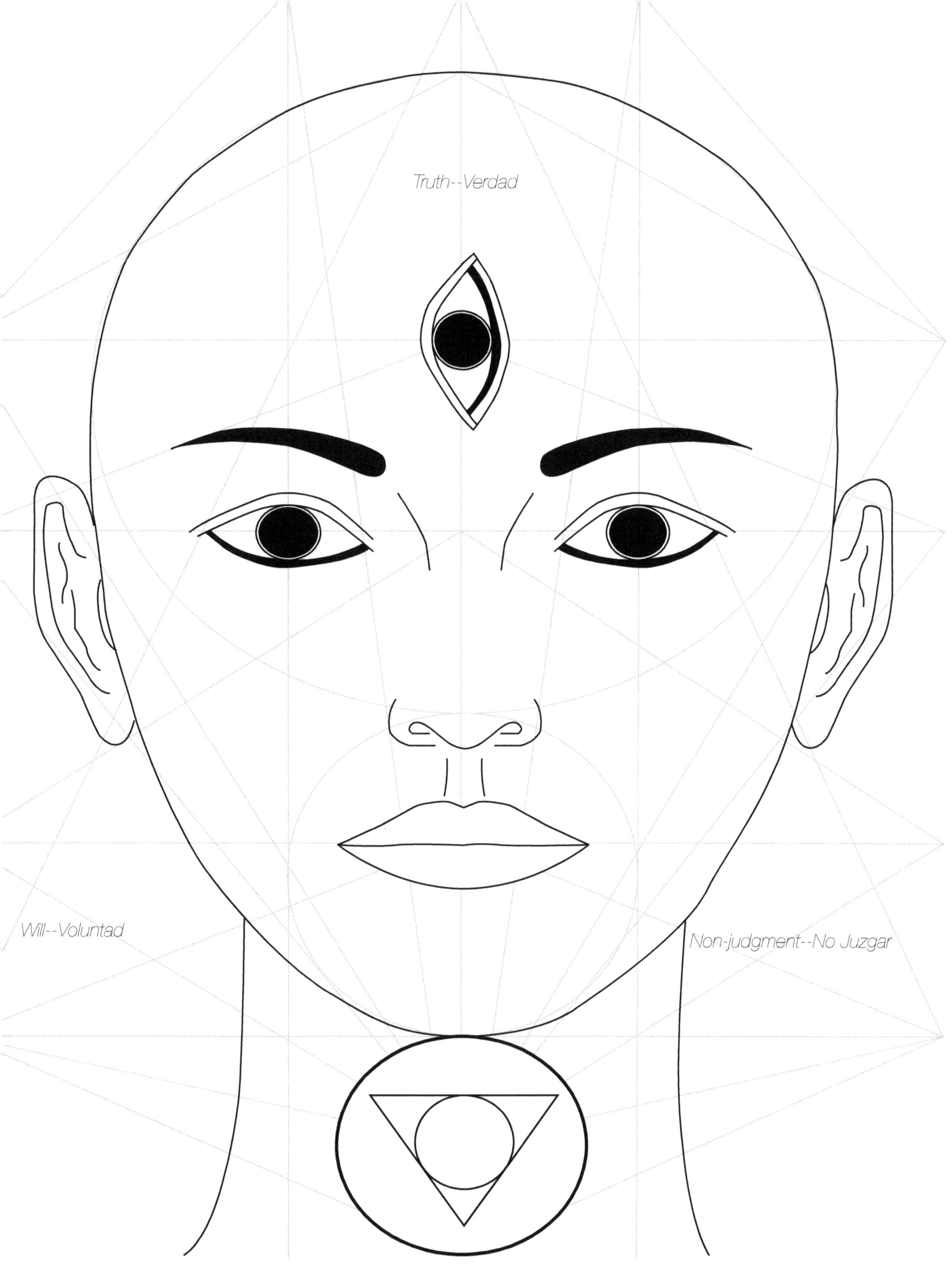

Truth--Verdad
Will--Voluntad
Non-judgment--No Juzgar

A J N A
The Third Eye

Sight and Insight

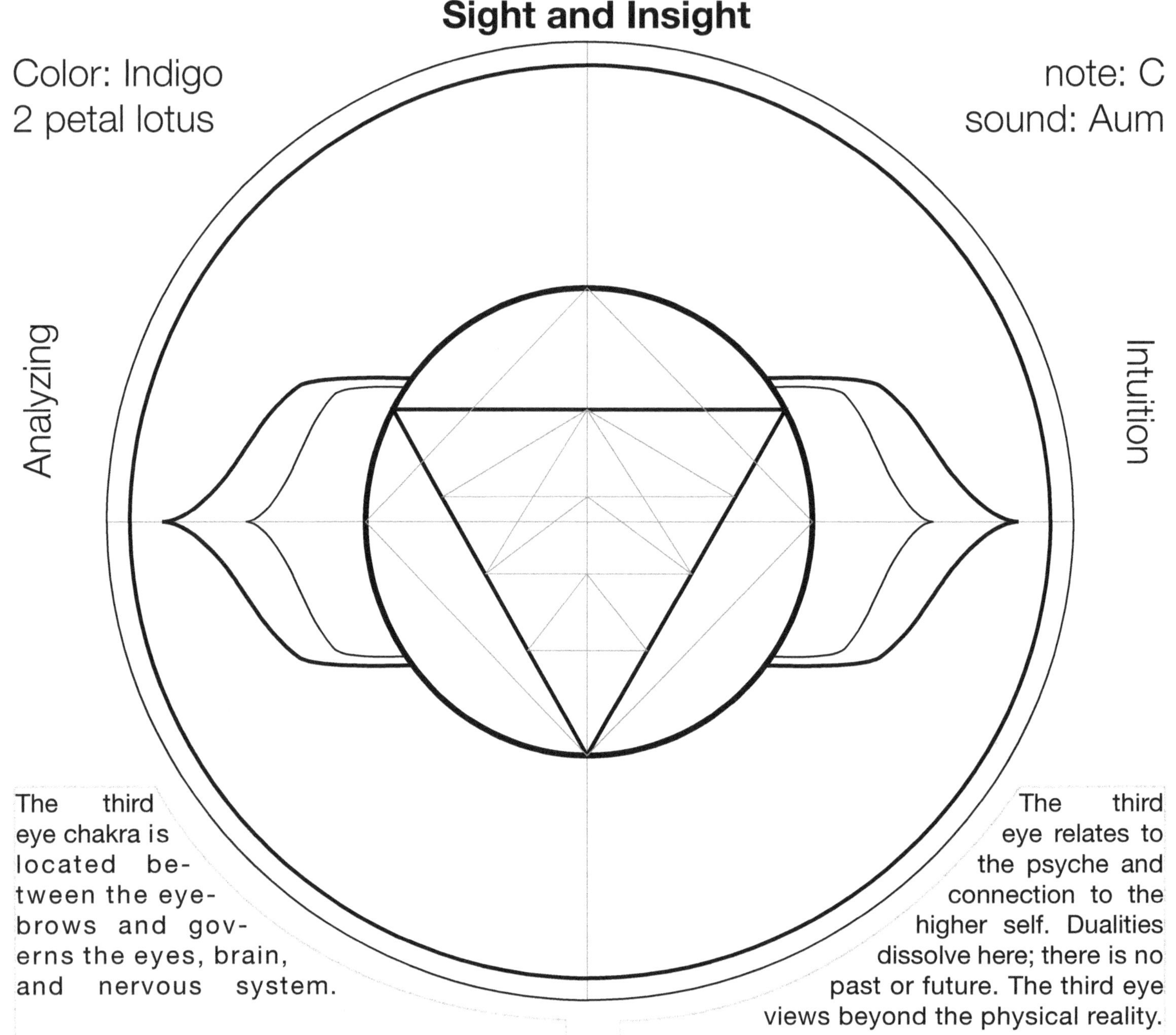

The third eye chakra is located between the eyebrows and governs the eyes, brain, and nervous system.

Anja oversees perception and imagination.

The sixth chakra is the eye of intuition and insight, the ability to see things as they really are, dissolving dualities and seeing the whole of the parts. Intuition is often referred to as a sixth sense and developing the third eye, also known as the **Sky Eye** or inner eye, is to cultivate a different kind of sense awareness.

The third eye relates to the psyche and connection to the higher self. Dualities dissolve here; there is no past or future. The third eye views beyond the physical reality.

Self-realization, beyond desires of the lower chakras, develops as the third eye is exercised.

Both the sixth and seventh chakras connect to the spirit realm. It is in this area of the upper chakras that one finds a new perspective, and connects to the higher self to find divine understanding and wisdom.

Epiphany--Epifania
Without Desire--Sin Deseo
Wisdom--Sabiduría

SAHASRARA
The Crown Chakra
Chimney to Other Dimensions

Color: Violet or white
1000 petal lotus

note: B
sound: Silence

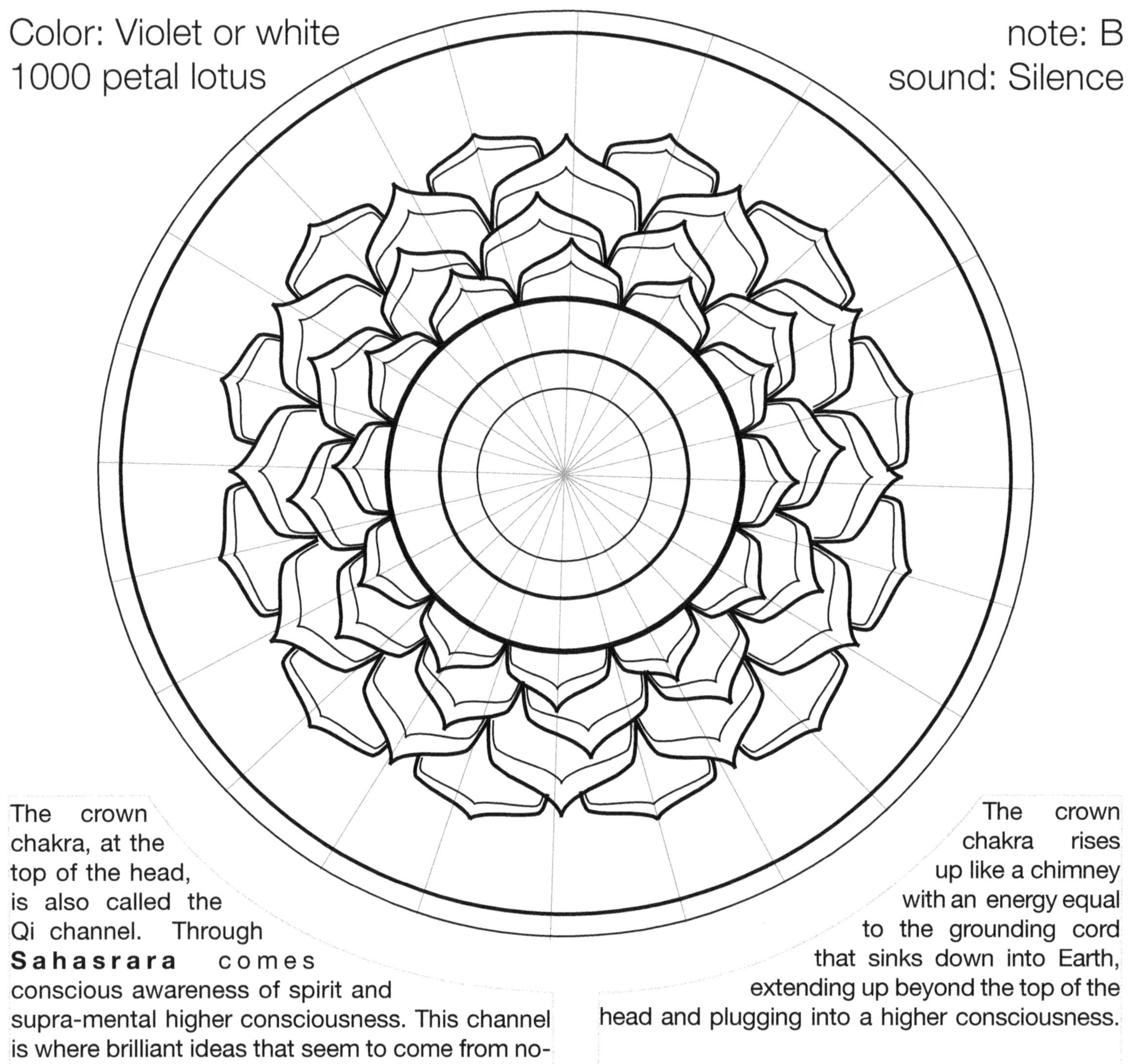

The crown chakra, at the top of the head, is also called the Qi channel. Through **Sahasrara** comes conscious awareness of spirit and supra-mental higher consciousness. This channel is where brilliant ideas that seem to come from no-where are transmitted. It is where the divine cavorts with the physical realm and brings illumination.

The seventh chakra oversees the cerebral cortex, skin, hormonal balance, and sleep.

The crown chakra rises up like a chimney with an energy equal to the grounding cord that sinks down into Earth, extending up beyond the top of the head and plugging into a higher consciousness.

The top of the seven spinal chakras is a place of selflessness and non-attachment to the physical realm. Here there is no inner or outer door, there is no duality, rather, there is only holism when one is connected to the Cosmic Consciousness.

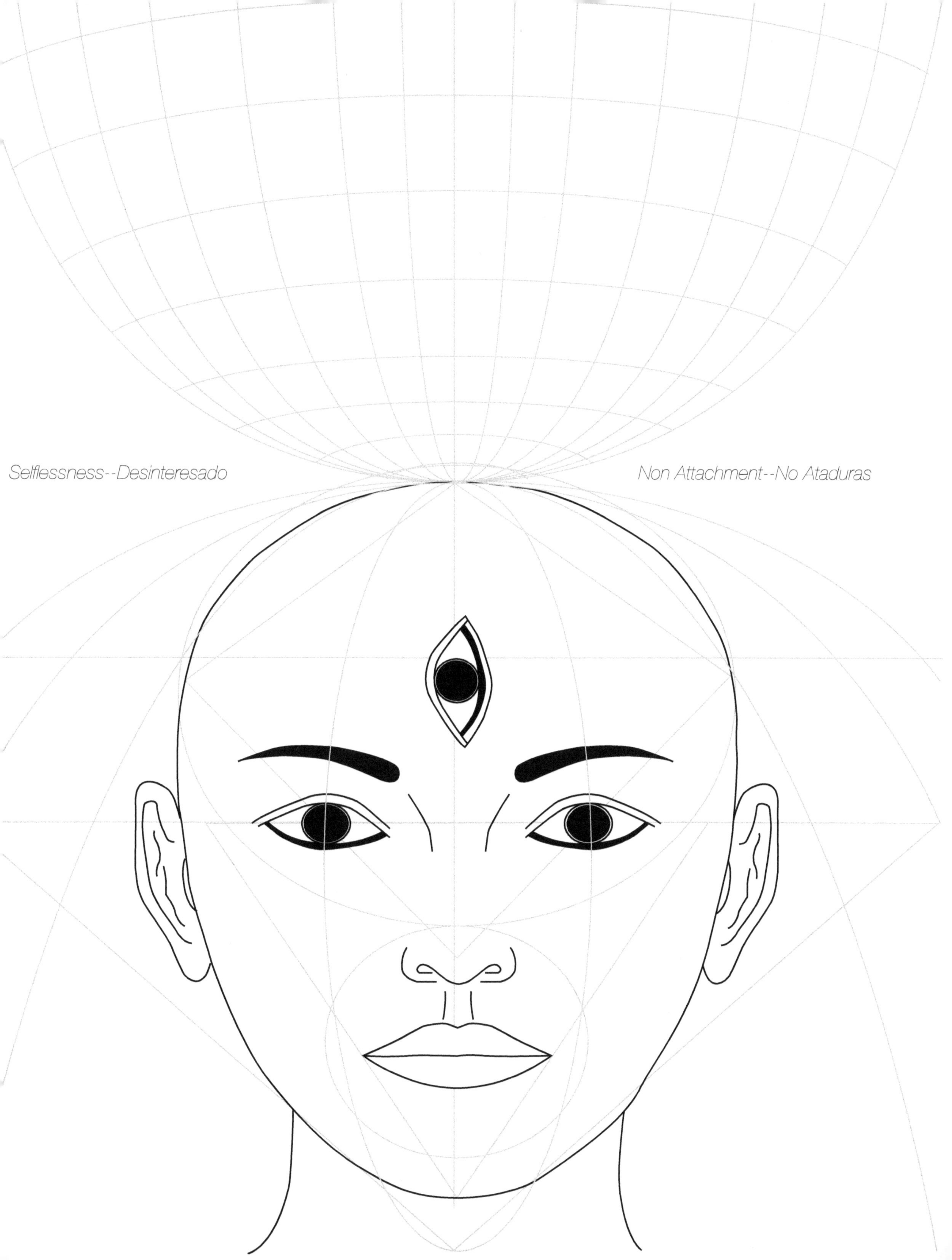

Selflessness--Desinteresado
Non Attachment--No Ataduras

Refinement & Distillation Process
in Traditional Medicine

Many traditions identify and map different energetic meridians of the body. In Traditional Chinese Medicine (TCM), each of the meridians is associated with an organ in the body, except for one: the Triple Warmer.

The Triple Warmer or Triple Burner, functions as a distillery in the physical body. In Qi Gong & Tai Chi, it resides within the three Dan Tien. This energetic alchemy heats and animates the body, beginning in the lower burner where a fire burns in the belly to digest; waste matter then exits the body as heat and distilled essence rise upward through the middle and upper burners, becoming more refined at each level, until rising up as ether.

Upper Burner: Area above the throat through crown of head, top three chakras
Shen – Spiritual Essence • Upper Dan Tien
The most refined essence of Qi rises up and transforms into sound and voice, sight and insight, continuing up the chimney of the crown into other dimensions.

Middle Burner: Area of heart and lungs, heart chakra
Chi – Energetic Essence • Middle Dan Tien
Energy is transformed in the area of the heart from the heat that rises up from the fire in lower chakras. The heart is the filter between the upper and lower chakras.

Lower Burner – Area below diaphragm through base of pelvis, lowest three chakras
Jing – Material Essence • Lower Dan Tien
The diaphragm acts as a bellows to the belly fire, where matter burns for energy and ash or waste returns to Earth to be recycled.

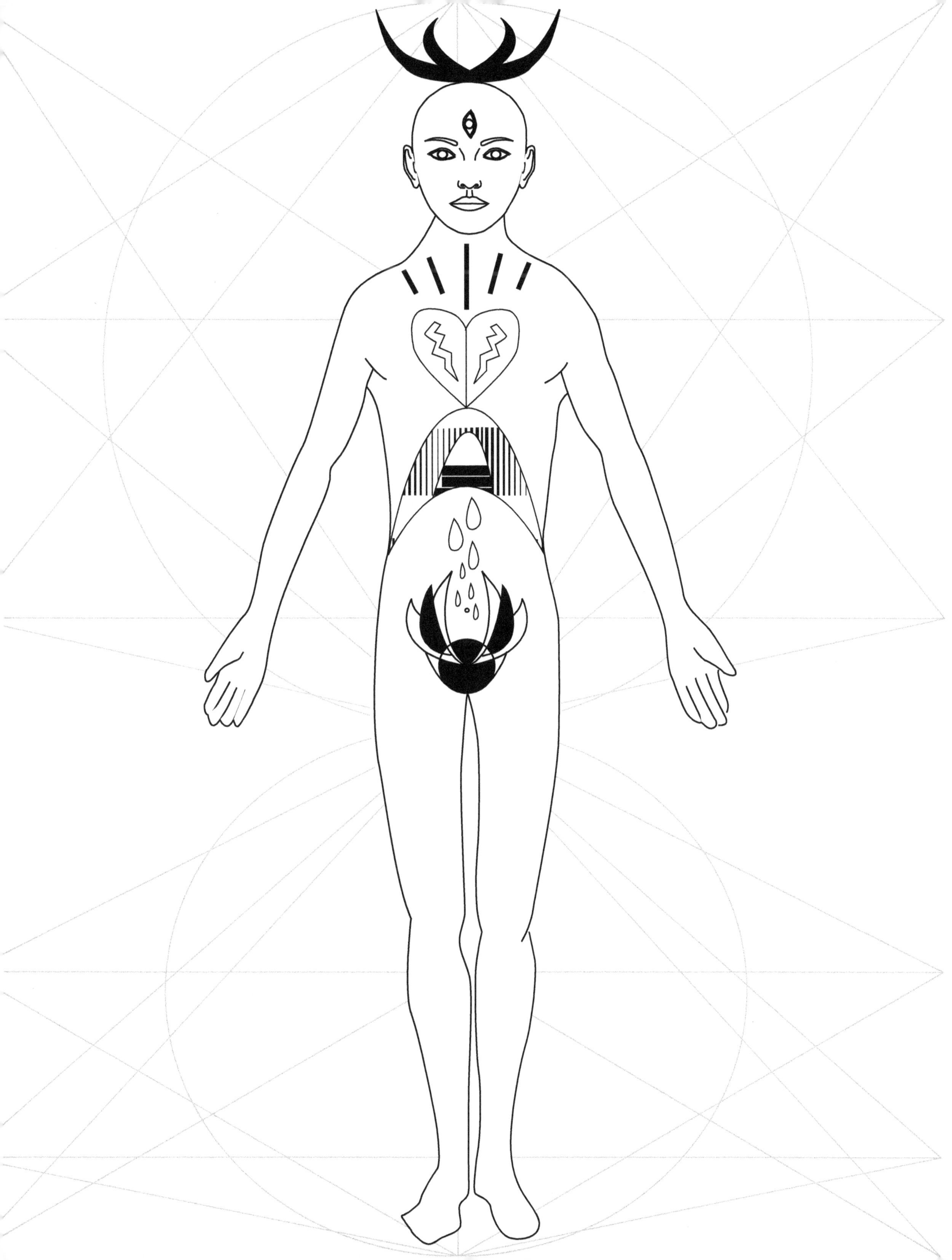

The Limbic & Endocrine Connection

It is possible that the limbic and endocrine systems hold the key to understanding the transmissions between the biological and energetic bodies. The limbic system is a part of the brain that influences the endocrine system and the autonomic nervous system. When stimulated by emotion, light, food, stress, or other forces, the endocrine glands release peptides and hormones which activate different aspects of the cells, effectively making the cells spin or move in unison.   Much research is currently being done in this area and scientists are not yet in agreement on exactly how the limbic system oversees the endocrine system, but some believe it is the link between understanding the quantum physics of the body.

The Crown	*Pineal Gland*	•The pineal gland creates light sensitive brain chemical melatonin, which oversees biological rhythms. •Appears to play a major role in sexual development, metabolism, and cycles such as sleep & reproduction.
The Third Eye	*Pituitary Gland*	•The pituitary gland releases hormones and peptides regulating homeostasis and stimulating other endocrine glands. •Considered a master gland and effects growth, blood pressure, and water regulation.
The Throat	*Thyroid and Parathyroid*	•The thyroid glands regulates metabolism, plays a role in growth and bone maintance, sexual and mental development. •The parathyroid glands regulate calcium and blood salt levels.
The Heart	*Thymus Gland*	•The thymus gland is a specialized organ of the immune system located above the heart which differentiates T-cells in the blood for immunity.
Solar Plexus	*Adrenals and Pancreas*	•These endocrine glands on top of kidneys are responsible for releasing hormones such as adrenaline and cortisol in the adrenals and insulin in the pancreas.
Sacral Chakra	*Sexual Organs*	•The ovaries and testicles create gametes for reproduction; spermatozoa in males and egg cells in females.
Root Chakra	*Spinal Column*	•The spinal column connects all the nerve ganglia which animate the physical body. •Oversees energy movement to limbs and throughout physical body.

QI EXERCISES
Embody Your Body

The Crown
SAHASRARA
Violet / Irridescent

The Third Eye
AJNA (AGNYA)
Indigo/Violet

The Throat
VISHUDDHI
Sea Blue / Cyan

The Heart
ANAHATA
New Growth Green

Solar Plexus
MANIPURA
Sunshine Yellow

The Sacral
SVADHISTHANA
Golden Orange

The Root
MULADHARA
Fiery Red Earth

Rainbow Breath:
- Get comfortable, center, and breathe.
- Ground yourself to Earth
- Imagine a column of bright white light coming down from the sky through the top of your head.
- Inhale and imagine the column of light penetrating the top of your head and illuminating a sparkling iridescent column through the core of your being.
- Follow the light column down and imagine each chakra center lighting up with your breath as you focus on it.
- Breathe and scan the chakras in both directions.

Cleanse and Align the Chakras:
- Stand, breathe, and ground yourself to Earth.
- Visualize your breath coming in through the top of your head and descending through your core chakra channel.
- Inhale deeply and condense your breath as deeply as you can, creating a ball of chi in the bowl of your pelvis.
- Bend forward at the waist and bend the knees slightly into a gentle squat, condensing the energy ball downward.
- As you exhale, stand up tall and shoot the ball of chi up from your pelvis bowl, through each of the chakras and out the top of the head.

Microcosmic Orbit:
- Sit or stand, breathe, ground yourself to Earth.
- Visualize your breath coming in through the top of your head, down the chakra column and exiting out the bottom of your pelvis.
- Create a circuit with your inhalation and exhalation, letting your breath exit out of the pelvis, and then drawing the exhalation breath up around you, and inhaling it back in through the top of your head.
- If you are standing, rock forward on the balls of your feet as you inhale and gently back on your heels as you exhale.
- You may find it useful to follow the visualization of your breath with your hand and arms.
- Place your tongue gently on the place where the upper palate and teeth meet.

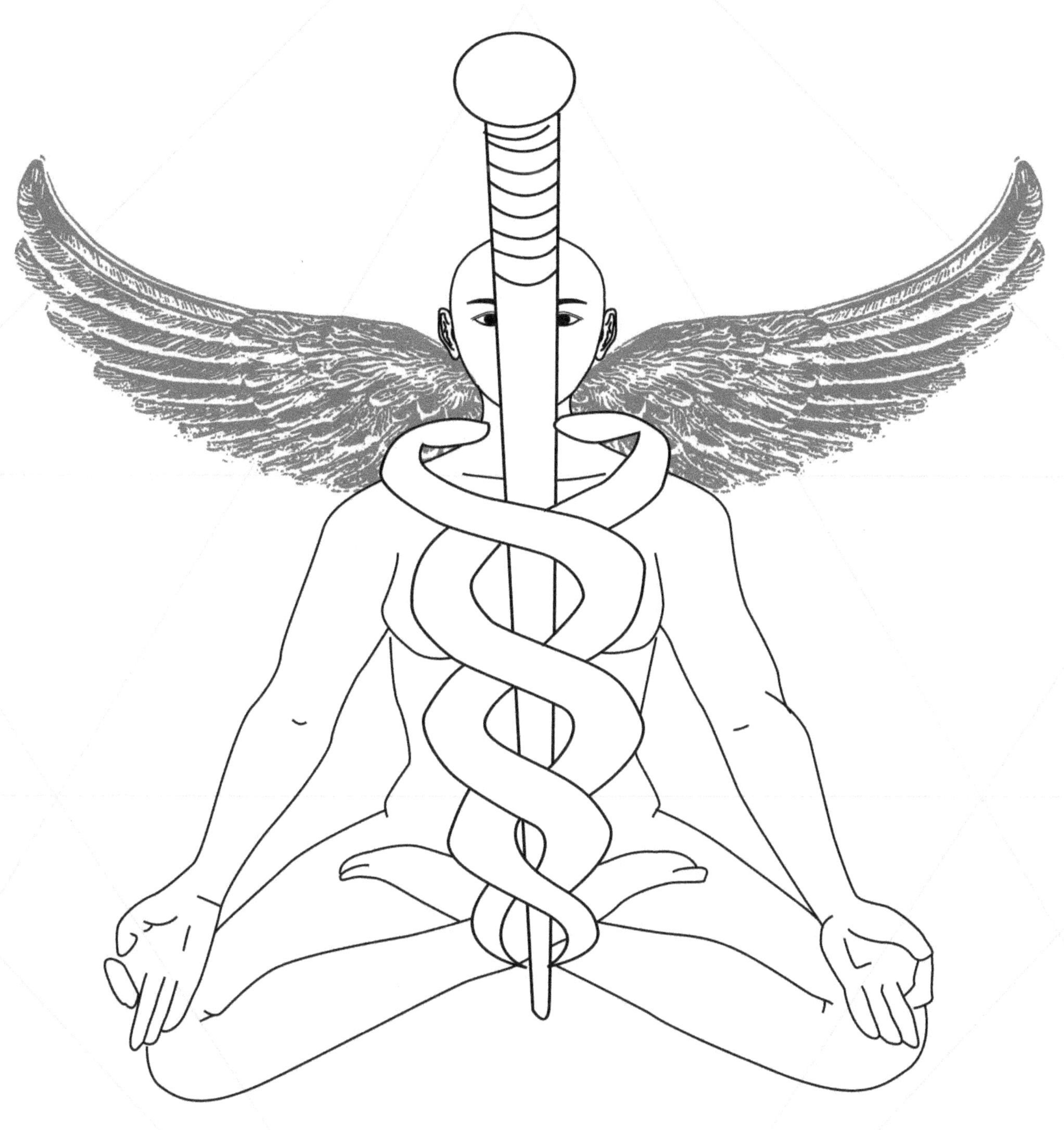

When one's energy flows freely, a person is open to the realm of all of the possibilities in the universe. Directly harness to the flow and consciousness of universal energy and find that the nascent potential to create is infinite. The Cosmic Consciousness is fecund with possibilities.

What do I want to create?

What was I born to do?

What makes my heart sing?

What gives me pleasure?

What is the right livelihood for me?

What do I dream?

What am I passionate about?

What belief system was I born into?

What do I want to manifest in this world?

What is my personal truth?

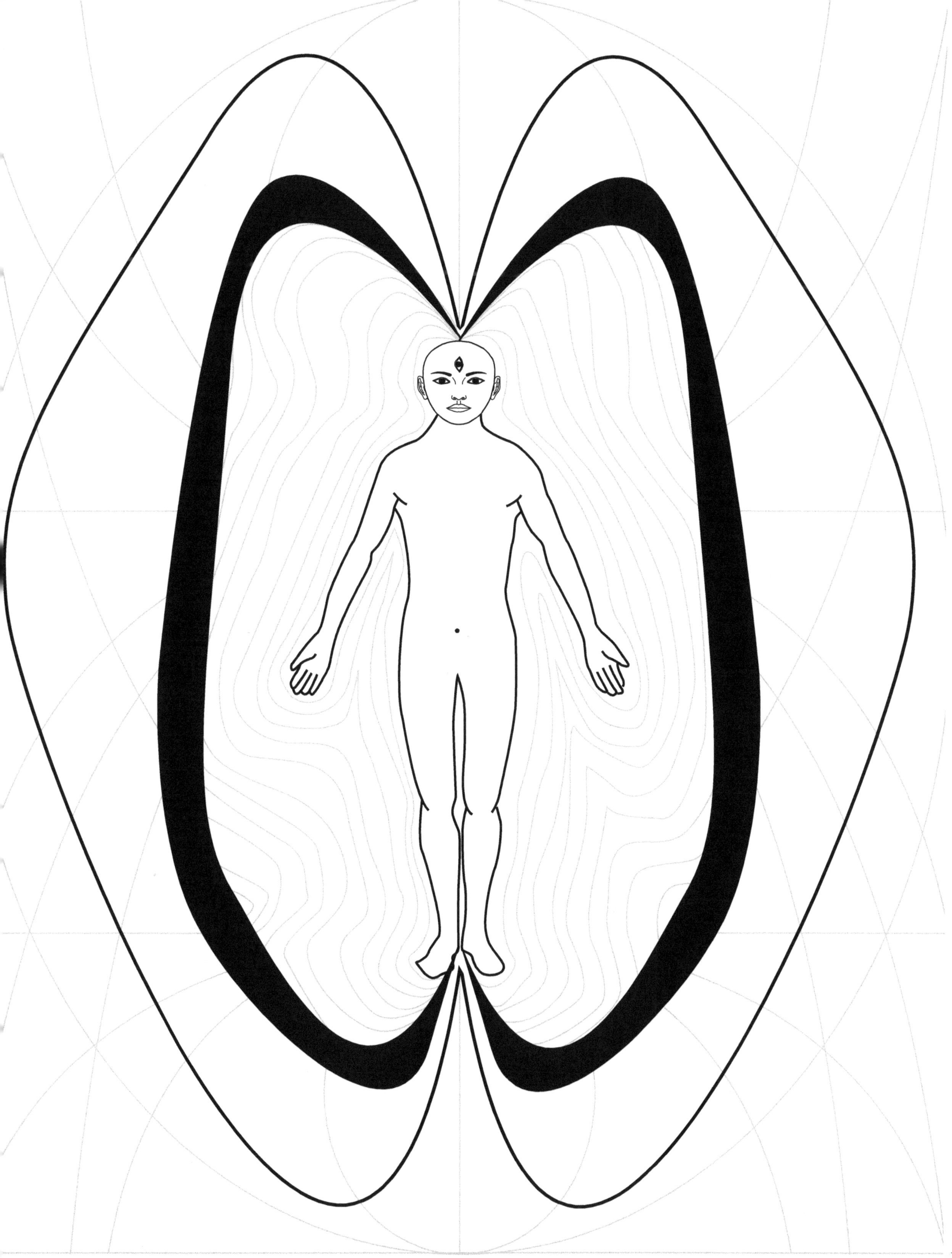

Our Wish for Your Becoming

Let these pages be a template for self expression. As you work through the pages of this book and shine your brightness into the unseen parts of you, be kind to yourself. Let your artworks develop naturally and without judgment, revealing insight and connecting you to your own wholeness. Color outside of the lines. Live outside the box. Just have fun. Life is Poetry.

About the Author & Illustrator

The inspiration for this book came in a dream that serendipitously led **Regina Marie** on a journey full of synchronicity. Regina's path has taken her around the world, as an artist and writer, yogini and healer, and as both a teacher and student of ancient wisdom. She is certified as a yoga and qi gong teacher, bodyworker, reiki master, sound healer and somatic wellness coach. She believes in the power of Om and vibration to align humans to remember, *we are the rainbow bridge*.

Legan Rooster is a cosmic creative artist who collaborated on this vision with the illustrations, book design and Spanish.

Regina and Legan met and worked on this project while both living in Hong Kong, far from their homelands of North and Central America, each one reaching within to find a sense of home abroad.

To find out more about Regina and ideas on how to use this book go to **www.inthebright.com**
Find us on social media @inthebright & @leganrooster